pie POPS

pie POPS

MARCIE BALLARD

Photographs by Susan Hayward

GIBBS SMITH
TO ENRICH AND INSPIRE HUMANKIND

First Edition
17 16 15 14 13   5 4 3 2 1

Text © 2013 Marcie Ballard
Photographs © 2013 Susan Hayward

Published by
Gibbs Smith
P.O. Box 667
Layton, Utah 84041

1.800.835.4993 orders
www.gibbs-smith.com

Designed by Rita Sowins / Sowins Design
Printed and bound in China
Gibbs Smith books are printed on either recycled, 100% post-consumer waste, FSC-certified papers or on paper produced from sustainable PEFC-certified forest/controlled wood source. Learn more at www.pefc.org.

Library of Congress Cataloging-in-Publication Data

Ballard, Marcie.
  Pie pops / Marcie Ballard ; photographs by Susan Barnson Hayward. — First edition.
      pages cm
  Includes index.
  ISBN 978-1-4236-3119-4
  1. Pies. 2. Craft sticks. I. Title.
  TX773.B28 2013
  641.86'52—dc23
                          2012050560

To the amazing women in my life,
who taught me if you work hard you
can have your pie and eat it too.

To the wonderful men in my life, who
keep me smiling and giggling, especially
when I have food in my teeth.

Contents

Basic Supplies & Tips

PIE POP DOUGH

- Don't make pie pop sizes too big because they might break apart. They should be a two or three bite dessert.

- Don't be afraid to use refrigerated pie dough. It makes the process incredibly easy. Pie pops are all about the pie filling.

- 1 9-inch pie dough will yield 10–12 pops if both tops and bottoms are used, and depending on size of dough cutouts.

- 1 9-inch pie dough will yield 20–24 pops if only bottoms are used, and depending on size of dough cutouts.

- When baking pie pops, keep an eye on baking time. You do not want to overcook them because they will become crunchy cookies instead of savory pie pops.

- Several simple recipes only take 20 minutes from start to finish.

PIE POP STICKS

- You can use various types of wooden sticks. These can be found at any craft store.
  Popsicle sticks
  Wavy craft sticks
  Hobby craft sticks (notched)
  Lollipop sticks

- To produce a colored pie pop stick, soak the sticks in water with food coloring added.

- Flat Popsicle sticks work better for thick pie pops.

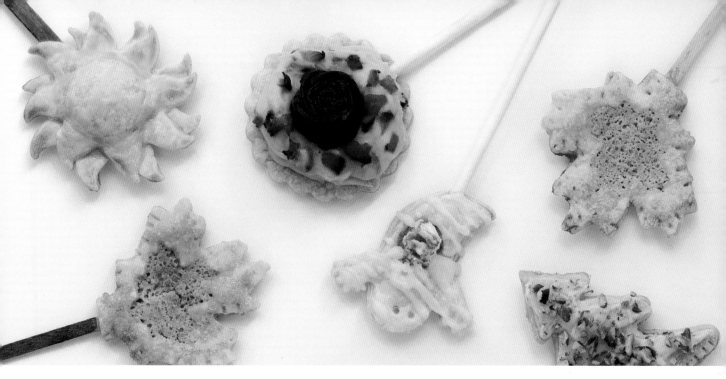

PIE POP SHAPES

- Creating the different shapes is the fun part. For a children's theme party, you can use cute animal shapes.

- Use various cookie cutter shapes to cut the pie pop dough. The standard size for most recipes will be $2\frac{1}{2}$ inches.

- Use various smaller 1-inch size cookie cutters to cut out the centers in the pie dough tops for some recipes.

- Cookie cutters can be found at any craft or kitchen specialty store.

- To sandwich sticks between dough shapes:
  Place cut dough bottoms on a lightly greased baking sheet. Push sticks into bottoms and prick dough with a fork. Add pie filling if placing it between dough layers, keeping the edges clear. Place tops over bottoms and crimp edges together with a fork.

PIE POP SHELLS

- Pie pops with filled dough shells set on top of sticks create a dramatic presentation.

- Use a 2 1/2-inch round cookie cutter to cut dough bottoms. Using mini tart tins turned upside-down or the outside cups of a lightly greased mini-muffin pan, mold the dough bottoms into cups.

- Bake on molds, first poking a hole in each dough center with a stick.

- Remove from oven and cool on a wire rack.

- To attach cup-shaped shells to tops of sticks:
    In a small microwave-safe bowl, melt 3 ounces white melting chocolate in microwave for 2 minutes stirring every 20 seconds until smooth. Secure sticks to each shell using the melted chocolate as an adhesive on the inside and outside of shell, and let the chocolate dry and harden for 15 minutes.

Basic Pie Dough

1 1/4 cups flour
Dash salt
1/2 teaspoon sugar
1/2 cup cold, unsalted butter cut into 1 inch cubes
3–4 tablespoons ice cold water

Add flour, salt, sugar, and butter to bowl of food processor. Using the chopping blade pulse 5–6 times, or until mixture becomes crumbly and coarse. Do not over pulse. Add 1 tablespoon of water at a time pulsing mixture after each addition until dough starts to slightly stick together but is still a little crumbly. Remember, too much water will make the dough too hard to work. You should be able to see small pieces of butter in the dough.

Remove the dough to a lightly floured surface. Mold mixture into a round disk, wrap in plastic, and place in refrigerator for at least 1 hour to set and chill. After dough has had time to chill, remove from refrigerator and let sit at room temperature for about 10 minutes. Roll dough out onto a lightly floured surface using a rolling pin that has been lightly dusted with flour. Roll out to 1/8-inch thickness.

powdered sugar icing

1 cup powdered sugar
¼ teaspoon vanilla
1 tablespoon milk

In a small bowl, mix all ingredients together until icing reaches a drizzle consistency.

VARIATIONS:

• Add 1–2 drops food coloring of choice to make a colored icing.

• Add 2 tablespoons unsweetened cocoa powder for a chocolate icing.

• Substitute 1 tablespoon orange or lemon juice in place of milk.

• Substitute ¼ teaspoon maple extract in place of vanilla.

• Substitute ¼ teaspoon almond extract in place of vanilla.

Bananas Foster

~ MAKES 15–20 ~

15–20 wooden candy sticks
5 small bananas
1 9-inch refrigerated pie dough, at room temperature
3 tablespoons butter
⅓ cup brown sugar
1 teaspoon cinnamon
¼ teaspoon nutmeg
1 teaspoon rum extract
1 cup vegetable oil
Powdered Sugar Icing (page 11)

Peel and cut bananas into 2-inch chunks. Insert sticks into bananas and place in freezer on a baking sheet for at least 15–20 minutes.

On a lightly floured surface, roll dough to ⅛-inch thickness. Use a 3-inch rectangle shaped cookie cutter to cut dough pieces. They should be large enough to wrap around the banana chunks. Set aside.

In a small saucepan, add the butter, sugar, cinnamon, and nutmeg. Stir and mix together until fully melted. Remove from heat, add the rum, and mix completely. Spread sugar mixture on the dough pieces, leaving the edges clean. Remove bananas from freezer, roll dough around bananas, and crimp edges together with a fork.

Heat oil in a large frying pan or use a deep fryer for faster results. Place banana pieces in oil using long tongs. Cook for 10–13 minutes, or until browned. Remove to paper towel and let cool slightly. Drizzle with Powdered Sugar Icing.

Banana Cream

18–20 wooden candy sticks
1 9-inch refrigerated pie dough, at room temperature
1 egg white, beaten
1/4 cup instant banana pudding mix
1 cup heavy cream
1 banana, peeled and sliced thin
Whipped topping

Preheat oven to 350 degrees.

Soak sticks in water for 15 minutes. On a lightly floured surface, roll dough out to 1/8-inch thickness. Use a 2 1/2-inch round cookie cutter to cut out dough tops and bottoms. Use a 1-inch cookie cutter shape to cut a center opening in tops. Place bottoms on a lightly greased baking sheet. Push sticks into bottoms and prick dough with a fork. Place tops over bottoms, crimp edges together with a fork, and brush with egg white. Bake for 12–13 minutes, or until slightly brown; do not overcook. Remove from oven and cool on a wire rack.

In a medium bowl, combine pudding mix and cream. Beat with an electric mixer on high speed until smooth and thick. Spoon mixture into a pastry bag with a large opening tip and pipe the filling onto each pop. Garnish with a banana slice and whipped topping. Refrigerate until ready to serve.

sensational spinach

~ MAKES 18-20 ~

18–20 wooden candy sticks
1 9-inch pie dough, at room temperature
1 egg white, beaten
2 cups fresh spinach, rinsed, dried, and torn into 1-inch pieces
1/2 cup dried cranberries, chopped
1/4 cup brown sugar
1 tablespoon lemon juice
Turbinado sugar

Preheat oven to 350 degrees.

Soak sticks in water for 15 minutes. On a lightly floured surface, roll dough out to $^1/_8$-inch thickness. Use a $2^1/_2$-inch cookie cutter shape to cut out dough tops and bottoms. Use a 1-inch cookie cutter shape to cut center opening in tops. Reserve cut out shapes. Place bottoms on a lightly greased baking sheet and brush with egg white. Push wooden sticks into bottoms and prick dough with a fork. Place several small pieces of spinach on each pie bottom.

In a small bowl, mix together cranberries, sugar, and lemon juice. Put 1 teaspoon of cranberry mixture on each spinach pile. Add dough top and crimp edges together with a fork. Place dough cutouts over cranberry filling. Brush tops with egg white and sprinkle with Turbinado sugar.

Bake for 13–15 minutes, or until lightly brown. Remove from oven and cool on a wire rack.

American Apple Pie

15–20 Popsicle sticks
1 9-inch refrigerated pie dough, at room temperature
1 (15-ounce) can apple pie filling, chopped
½ teaspoon cinnamon
¼ teaspoon nutmeg
Pinch ground cloves, if desired

Preheat oven to 350 degrees.

Soak sticks in water for 15 minutes. On a lightly floured surface, roll dough out to ⅛-inch thickness. Use a 3-inch apple shaped cookie cutter, or 3-inch round cookie cutter to cut out dough bottoms. Combine left over dough pieces and reserve for later. Place bottoms on a lightly greased baking sheet. Push sticks into bottoms and prick dough with a fork.

In a small bowl, combine pie filling and spices. Place a small spoonful of apple mixture in the center of each bottom. Keep the edges clear and don't overload the dough.

On a lightly floured surface, roll out leftover dough to ⅛-inch thickness. Use a butter knife or fluted dough cutter to cut ¼ inch strips to create a lattice layer for top of the pie pops. Layer dough strips in a basket weave pattern over apple filling and crimp edges together with a fork. Bake for 14–16 minutes, or until golden brown. Remove from oven and cool on a wire rack.

Dark Chocolate Fudge

20–25 Popsicle sticks
1 9-inch refrigerated pie dough, at room temperature
1 egg white, beaten
1 (3.9 ounce) box chocolate fudge instant pudding mix
1$\frac{1}{2}$ cups heavy cream
1 cup dark chocolate chips
$\frac{5}{8}$ cup sweetened condensed milk
2 tablespoons butter

Preheat oven to 350 degrees.

Soak sticks in water for 15 minutes. On a lightly floured surface, roll dough out to $\frac{1}{8}$-inch thickness. Use a 3-inch rectangular shape cookie cutter to cut out dough bottoms. Place bottoms on a lightly greased baking sheet. Push sticks into bottoms and use leftover dough to cover tips of sticks. Brush dough with egg white and prick with a fork. Bake for 11–13 minutes, or until lightly browned. Remove from oven and cool on a wire rack.

In a medium bowl, combine pudding mix and cream. Beat with an electric mixer on high speed until smooth and thick. Spoon pudding into a pastry bag with a large opening tip and pipe onto pops. Place in refrigerator to chill.

In a small microwave-safe bowl, combine chocolate chips, condensed milk, and butter. Heat in microwave on high for 2 minutes stirring every 20 seconds until mixture is smooth. Pour into candy mold of choice and place in the freezer for 10 minutes to set. Pop candy pieces out and garnish tops of pie pops. Refrigerate until ready to serve.

caramel apple pie

15–20 wooden candy sticks
1 9-inch refrigerated pie dough, at room temperature
1 Granny Smith apple, cut into 1-inch slivers
Cinnamon
1 egg white, beaten
Turbinado sugar
1 cup brown sugar
1/2 cup half-and-half
1/4 cup butter, softened
2 teaspoons vanilla extract

Preheat oven to 350 degrees.

Soak sticks in water for 15 minutes. On a lightly floured surface, roll dough out to 1/8-inch thickness. Use a 3-inch cookie cutter shape to cut out dough tops and bottoms. Use a 1-inch cookie cutter shape to cut a center opening in tops. Place bottoms on a lightly greased baking sheet. Push sticks into bottoms and top each one with a few apple slices; dust with cinnamon.

Place tops on each apple mound and crimp edges together with a fork. Brush tops with egg white and sprinkle with Turbinado sugar. Bake for 16–18 minutes, or until golden brown. Remove from oven and cool on a wire rack.

In a medium saucepan, combine brown sugar and half-and-half over medium heat, stirring until sugar dissolves. Add butter and vanilla bringing to a simmer on low heat stirring constantly with a whisk for 1 minute. The consistency will be smooth and slightly thick. Drizzle caramel over pops before serving.

Just Peachy

~ MAKES 15–20 ~

15–20 wooden sticks
1 9-inch refrigerated pie dough, at room temperature
1 (14-ounce) can peach pie filling, chopped
½ teaspoon cinnamon
¼ teaspoon nutmeg
1 egg white, beaten
Turbinado sugar
Powdered Sugar Icing (page 11), if desired

Preheat oven to 350 degrees.

Soak sticks in water for 15 minutes. On a lightly floured surface, roll dough out to $^1/_8$-inch thickness. Use a $2^1/_2$-inch cookie cutter shape to cut out dough tops and bottoms. Use a 1-inch cookie cutter shape to cut out a center opening in tops. Place bottoms on a lightly greased baking sheet. Push wooden sticks into bottoms and prick with a fork.

In a small bowl, combine the pie filling and spices. Drop a small spoonful of peach mixture on each bottom. Place tops over each peach mound and crimp edges together with a fork. Brush tops with egg white and sprinkle with Turbinado sugar. Bake for 13–15 minutes, or until slightly golden brown. Remove from oven and cool on a wire rack. Drizzle with Powdered Sugar Icing, if using.

CRazy GOOd CRaisin

~ MAKES 10-12 ~

10–12 Popsicle sticks

¼ cup sugar

1 tablespoon flour

Pinch salt

1 teaspoon cinnamon

½ teaspoon nutmeg

1 teaspoon ground cloves

¼ teaspoon vanilla extract

2 tablespoons lemon juice

⅓ cup raisins

½ cup dried cranberries, chopped

1 9-inch refrigerated pie dough, at room temperature

1 egg white, beaten

Turbinado sugar

Pink food coloring

Powdered Sugar Icing (page 11)

Preheat oven to 350 degrees.

Soak sticks in water for 15 minutes. In a medium microwave-safe bowl, mix sugar, flour, salt, and spices together. Add vanilla and lemon juice and stir together until sugar has dissolved. Add raisins and cranberries. Cook in microwave on high for about 3 minutes, stirring at least once. Remove and set aside.

On a lightly floured surface, roll dough out to ⅛-inch thickness. Use a 2½-inch cookie cutter shape to cut out dough tops and bottoms. Place bottoms on a lightly greased baking sheet and push sticks into bottoms. Drop a small spoonful of mixture on each bottom, cover with top, and crimp edges together with a fork. Cut vents or slits in tops with a sharp knife, brush with egg white, and sprinkle with Turbinado sugar. Bake for 12–14 minutes. Remove from oven and cool on a wire rack.

Add food coloring to Powdered Sugar Icing to achieve desired color and drizzle over pops.

Chocoholic

~ MAKES 20–25 ~

20–25 wooden sticks
1 9-inch refrigerated pie dough, at room temperature
4 ounces melting chocolate
¼ cup instant chocolate pudding mix
1 cup heavy cream
½ cup mini chocolate chips

Preheat oven to 350 degrees.

Soak sticks in water for 15 minutes. On a lightly floured surface, roll dough to ⅛-inch thickness. Use a 2½-inch cookie cutter shape to cut out dough bottoms. Place on a lightly greased baking sheet. Push sticks into bottoms and prick with a fork. Use leftover dough to cover tips of sticks. Bake for 12–13 minutes; just long enough to cook dough and set shape. Remove from oven and cool on a wire rack.

In a small microwave-safe bowl, melt chocolate in microwave on high for 2 minutes stirring every 20 seconds until smooth. Drizzle over pie pops or cover completely.

In a medium bowl, combine pudding mix and cream. Beat with an electric mixer on high speed until smooth and thick. Spoon pudding into a pastry bag with a large opening tip and pipe onto each pop. Garnish with chocolate chips. Refrigerate until ready to serve.

Lemon Pinnoli

14–16 white lollipop sticks
1 9-inch refrigerated pie dough, at room temperature
1 egg white, beaten
¼ teaspoon nutmeg
2 ounces cream cheese, softened
¼ cup powdered sugar
¾ cup ricotta cheese
1 teaspoon vanilla extract
3 teaspoons lemon juice
Powdered sugar
½ teaspoon saffron (optional)

Preheat oven to 375 degrees.

On a lightly floured surface, roll dough out to $^1/_8$-inch thickness. Use a $2\,^1/_2$-inch triangle cookie cutter shape to cut out dough tops and bottoms. Place bottoms on a lightly greased baking sheet and push sticks into bottom triangle point. Triangle will be upside down, similar to a martini glass. Brush with egg white and sprinkle with nutmeg.

Cut out 14–16 3-inch squares of aluminum foil. Roll each square and place in center of dough bottoms. Place tops over foil pieces and lightly crimp side edges together. Leave dough open at top to be able to remove the foil after baking. Bake for 8 minutes to set the shape. Remove from oven and gently remove foil pieces. Reduce heat to 350 degrees and bake another 3–4 minutes, or until golden brown. Remove from oven and cool on a wire rack.

In a medium bowl, mix cream cheese and sugar together with an electric mixer. Add the ricotta, vanilla, and lemon juice and mix until well combined. Spoon mixture into a pastry bag with a medium opening tip and fill each pie pop. Garnish with powdered sugar and saffron. Refrigerate until ready to serve.

APPle HavaRti

15–20 Popsicle sticks
1 9-inch refrigerated pie dough, at room temperature
¼ of a tart apple, peeled and diced
1 teaspoon cinnamon
2 tablespoons brown sugar
10–12 small slices Havarti cheese
Fresh dill

Preheat oven to 350 degrees.

Soak sticks in water for 15 minutes. On a lightly floured surface, roll dough out to $1/8$-inch thickness. Use a $2^1/2$-inch cookie cutter shape to cut out dough tops and bottoms. Use a 1-inch cookie cutter shape to cut a center opening in dough tops. Place bottoms on a lightly greased baking sheet. Push sticks into bottoms.

In a small bowl, combine apple pieces, cinnamon, and sugar. Drop a small spoonful of apple on each dough bottom, cover with dough top, and crimp edges together with a fork. Bake for 10–11 minutes. Remove from oven and immediately top with cheese. Garnish with a pinch of dill.

Razzleberry

~ MAKES 12–14 ~

12–14 Popsicle sticks
1 9-inch refrigerated pie dough, at room temperature
1 cup fresh raspberries
¼ cup sugar
1 egg white, beaten
Turbinado sugar
Powdered Sugar Icing (page 11)

Preheat oven to 350 degrees.

Soak sticks in water for 15 minutes. On a lightly floured surface, roll dough out to $\frac{1}{8}$-inch thickness. Use a $2\frac{1}{2}$-inch cookie cutter shape to cut out dough tops and bottoms. Use a 1-inch cookie cutter shape to cut out center opening in dough tops. Reserve cutout shapes. Place bottoms on a lightly greased baking sheet. Push sticks into bottoms and prick dough with a fork.

In a small bowl, mix the raspberries and sugar together. Make sure raspberries are in smaller pieces. Place a small amount of filling in center of each bottom making sure not to overfill, or filling will boil out. Be sure to leave a clean edge around the dough for a good closure. Cover with tops and crimp edges together with a fork. Place reserved dough shapes over center opening. Brush with egg white and sprinkle with Turbinado sugar.

Bake for 15–16 minutes, or until golden brown. Keep a watch to make sure pie filling doesn't boil out. Remove from oven and cool on a wire rack. Drizzle with Powdered Sugar Icing while still warm.

Orange Crème Brûlée

~ MAKES 20–25 ~

20–25 wooden candy sticks

1 9-inch refrigerated pie dough, at room temperature

3 ounces white melting chocolate, optional

2 tablespoons cornstarch

1 cup heavy cream

1 cup sweetened condensed milk

2 egg yolks, beaten

1 teaspoon orange extract

1 tablespoon butter

1/4 cup sugar

Whipped cream

Preheat oven to 350 degrees.

Soak sticks in water for 15 minutes. On a lightly floured surface, roll dough out to 1/8-inch thickness. Use a 2 1/2-inch flower shaped cookie cutter to cut dough bottoms. Using the outside cups of a lightly greased mini-muffin pan or individual mini tart tins, mold the bottoms into flower-shaped cups. Poke each wooden stick into center of dough, using the leftover dough to help secure sticks to pie shell. Remove top oven racks to allow for baking space. Bake for 14–15 minutes, or until slightly golden brown. Remove from oven and cool on a wire rack.

If sticks are not adhering firmly to pie shells, use white chocolate to attach them with the method described on page 10. Stick pops into a tall box or styrofoam base that has been prepared with small hole openings.

In a medium saucepan, combine the cornstarch and cream over medium-low heat. Whisk in the milk, egg yolks, and orange extract; add butter. Cook and stir until a slight boil is reached; mixture should be thick. Remove from heat and chill for about 30 minutes in refrigerator. Spoon the filling into each flower cup, leaving a slight well in the crème for the sugar to sit. Sprinkle about 1/2 teaspoon of sugar into filling wells. Using a crème brûlée torch, heat the sugar until it starts to caramelize. Garnish with whipped topping before serving. Refrigerate any leftover pops.

Spiced Pumpkin

~ MAKES 15-20 ~

12–15 Popsicle sticks
Red food coloring
1 9-inch refrigerated pie dough, at room temperature
1 cup canned pumpkin puree
2 tablespoons cornstarch
½ cup brown sugar
1 teaspoon cinnamon
½ teaspoon ground ginger
¼ teaspoon ground nutmeg
¼ teaspoon ground cloves
1 tablespoon cream cheese, softened
¼ cup heavy cream
Chocolate shavings or sprinkles, optional

Preheat oven to 350 degrees.

Soak sticks in water that has been colored with red food coloring for 15 minutes. On a lightly floured surface, roll dough out to ⅛-inch thickness. Use a 2½-inch pumpkin shaped cookie cutter to cut out dough tops and bottoms. Use a 1-inch cookie cutter shape to cut a center opening in dough tops. Place bottoms on a lightly greased baking sheet and push sticks into bottoms.

In a small bowl, mix together the pumpkin, cornstarch, sugar, and spices. Place about ½ tablespoon of pumpkin mixture in center of each bottom. Place tops over pumpkin and crimp edges together with a fork. Bake for 15–17 minutes, or until golden brown. Remove from oven and cool on a wire rack.

In a small bowl, whip cream cheese and cream together with a mixer on high speed until thick. Garnish each pop with a dollop of cream and chocolate shavings.

Aloha

14–16 wooden craft sticks
1 9-inch refrigerated pie dough, at room temperature
1 egg white, beaten
3 ounces cream cheese, softened
1/4 cup shredded coconut, divided
1/2 cup cream of coconut (do not shake can before opening)
1/4 cup crushed pineapple, drained
Whipped topping

Preheat oven to 350 degrees.

Soak sticks in water for 15 minutes. On a lightly floured surface, roll dough out to 1/8-inch thickness. Use a 2 1/2-inch pineapple shaped cookie cutter to cut out dough tops and bottoms. Place bottoms on a lightly greased baking sheet and push sticks into bottoms. Prick dough with a fork and brush with egg white.

Cut out 14–16 3-inch squares of aluminum foil. Crimp or roll each piece and place in center of dough bottoms. Cut the top part off of dough tops and use a knife to score a pattern on fronts. Place tops over bottoms and use a fork to crimp edges together. Bake for 13–15 minutes, or until golden brown. Remove from oven and cool on a wire rack. Remove foil pieces and discard.

Place half of coconut on a separate baking sheet and toast in oven for about 3 minutes, or until lightly browned.

In a medium bowl, combine cream cheese and cream of coconut together with an electric mixer on high until well blended. Mix in crushed pineapple and remaining untoasted coconut. Add mixture to a pastry bag with a medium opening tip and pipe filling inside each pie pop. Garnish with a small dollop of whipped topping and toasted coconut. Refrigerate until ready to serve.

Lumberjack

18–20 wooden sucker sticks
1 9-inch refrigerated pie dough, at room temperature
5 strips crispy bacon
1 cup powdered sugar
¼ teaspoon vanilla extract
1 teaspoon maple extract
½ cup heavy cream
¼ cup chopped pecans

Preheat oven to 350 degrees.

Soak sticks in water for 15 minutes. On a lightly floured surface, roll dough out to ⅛-inch thickness. Use a 2½-inch cookie cutter shape to cut dough bottoms. Place bottoms on a lightly greased baking sheet and prick dough with a fork. Use any leftover dough to cover tips of sticks. Bake for 14–16 minutes, or until lightly brown. Remove from oven and cool on a wire rack.

Chop cooked bacon into small pieces and place desired amounts of bacon on each pie pop. In a medium bowl, beat together sugar, vanilla, and maple extract with an electric mixer. Add cream and whip to a thick consistency. Spoon frosting into a pastry bag with a small tip and pipe onto pops. Sprinkle with chopped pecans.

Lemon Meringue

20–25 white lollipop sticks
1 9-inch refrigerated pie dough, at room temperature
1 egg white, beaten
1/4 cup instant lemon pudding mix
1 cup half-and-half
2 egg whites, at room temperature
1/2 cup sugar (1/4 cup sugar for each egg white)
1/2 teaspoon vanilla extract
Zest of 1 lemon

Preheat oven to 350 degrees.

On a lightly floured surface, roll dough out to 1/8-inch thickness. Use a 2 1/2-inch round cookie cutter to cut dough bottoms. Using the outside cups of a lightly greased mini-muffin pan or individual mini tart tins, mold the dough bottoms into cups. Brush with egg white. Poke a hole in each dough center with a stick. You will be attaching the sticks later in the process. Bake for 12–14 minutes, or until slightly golden brown. Remove from oven and cool on a wire rack.

In a small microwave-safe bowl, melt chocolate in microwave for 2 minutes stirring every 20 seconds until smooth. Secure sticks to each shell using the melted chocolate as an adhesive on the inside and outside of shell, and let the chocolate dry and harden for 15 minutes.

Stick pops into a tall box or styrofoam base that has been prepared with small hole openings. In a medium bowl, beat together pudding mix and half-and-half with an electric mixer until thickened. Spoon mixture into each pop. Don't add too much or they will become too heavy and fall apart.

In a medium bowl, beat egg whites on high until soft peaks start to form. Add sugar and vanilla gradually. Continue to mix until sugar has dissolved and stiff peaks have formed. Top each pop with 1 tablespoon of meringue. Using a cooling rack to hold pie pops upright, carefully place pops back in oven under the broiler and toast meringue until golden brown. Garnish with lemon zest and serve immediately. Refrigerate any leftover pops.

Ginger Snap Dragon

~ MAKES 15–18 ~

15–18 wooden sticks
1 9-inch refrigerated pie dough, at room temperature
1 egg white, beaten
1 1/4 teaspoons ground ginger, divided
1/2 cup flour
1/4 cup brown sugar
1/2 teaspoon cinnamon
3 tablespoons unsulphured molasses
Powdered Sugar Icing (page 11)

Preheat oven to 350 degrees.

Soak sticks in water for 15 minutes. On a lightly floured surface, roll dough out to 1/8-inch thickness. Use a 2 1/2-inch flower shaped cookie cutter to cut out dough tops and bottoms. Use a 1-inch flower cookie cutter to cut out a center opening in dough tops. Place bottoms on a lightly greased baking sheet and push sticks into bottoms. Brush with egg white, prick dough with fork, and sprinkle with 1/4 teaspoon ginger.

In a medium bowl, mix together flour, sugar, cinnamon, and remaining ginger. Add molasses and mix until well combined; mixture will be somewhat thick. Place 1 teaspoon of mixture in the center of each bottom. Press down with a spoon to flatten slightly. Add tops and crimp edges together with a fork. Bake for 14–16 minutes, or until golden brown. Remove from oven and cool on a wire rack. Drizzle with Powdered Sugar Icing.

J'Adore

12–14 wooden sticks
1 9-inch refrigerated pie dough, at room temperature
1 egg white, beaten
Turbinado sugar
¼ cup sugar
2 tablespoons cornstarch
½ cup water
½ (3.0-ounce) box strawberry gelatin
½ cup chopped strawberries
Whipped topping

Preheat oven to 350 degrees.

Soak sticks in water for 15 minutes. On a lightly floured surface, roll dough out to ⅛-inch thickness. Use a 2½-inch heart shaped cookie cutter to cut out dough tops and bottoms. Place bottoms on a lightly greased baking sheet and push sticks into bottom point of heart shaped dough. Brush with egg white and prick dough with a fork.

Cut 12–14 2-inch squares of aluminum foil. Roll each piece and place in center of dough bottoms. Place tops over foil and crimp edges together with a fork, leaving the top of the heart open. Brush tops with egg white and generously sprinkle with Turbinado sugar. Bake for 14–15 minutes, or until slightly golden brown. Remove from oven and cool on a wire rack. Remove foil pieces.

In a medium saucepan, stir sugar and cornstarch together over medium heat until sugar has dissolved. Add water a little at time stirring constantly until it reaches a boil. Remove from heat and sprinkle the gelatin over the top. Fold in strawberries.

Use a small spoon to fill each pie pop with the strawberry mixture. Top with a small dollop of whipped topping. Refrigerate until ready to serve.

Cappuccino Crème

~ MAKES 20–25 ~

20–25 wooden craft sticks
1 9-inch refrigerated pie dough, at room temperature
1 egg white, beaten
1 cup heavy cream
4 tablespoons Maxwell House Toasted Hazelnut flavored Cappuccino
Whipped topping
Cinnamon

Preheat oven to 350 degrees.

Soak sticks in water for 15 minutes. On a lightly floured surface, roll dough out to $1/8$-inch thickness. Use a 3-inch coffee cup shaped cookie cutter to cut dough bottoms. Place bottoms on a lightly greased baking sheet and push sticks into bottoms. Use leftover dough to cover tips of sticks. Brush with egg white and prick dough with a fork. Bake for 13–14 minutes, or until slightly golden brown. Remove from oven and cool on a wire rack.

In a medium bowl, beat together the cream and flavored cappuccino with an electric mixer on high speed until thickened. Top each pop with flavored cream and a dollop of whipped topping; dust with cinnamon. Refrigerate until ready to serve.

ROCKY ROad

~ MAKES 20-25 ~

20–25 wooden sticks
1 9-inch refrigerated pie dough, at room temperature
1 egg white, beaten
1 (4-ounce) box chocolate instant pudding mix
1 cup cold half-and-half
1 1/2 cups whipped topping, divided
1 cup mini marshmallows, about 20 pieces
3/4 cup chopped almonds, divided

Preheat oven to 350 degrees.

Soak sticks in water for 15 minutes. On a lightly floured surface, roll dough out to $1/8$-inch thickness. Use a $2^{1}/_{2}$-inch cookie cutter shape to cut dough bottoms. Place bottoms on a lightly greased baking sheet and push sticks into bottoms. Use leftover dough to cover tips of sticks. Brush dough with egg white and prick with a fork. Bake for 14–15 minutes, or until golden brown. Remove from oven and cool on a wire rack.

In a large bowl, combine pudding mix and half-n-half and beat together with an electric mixer on high speed until thickened. Fold in 1 cup whipped topping and mix in marshmallows and $1/2$ cup almonds. Let chill in refrigerator for 15 minutes.

Spoon about 1 tablespoon of pudding mixture onto each pie pop. Garnish with remaining whipped topping and remaining almonds. Refrigerate until ready to serve.

Root Beer Float

~ MAKES 20–25 ~

20–25 wooden sticks
1 9-inch refrigerated pie dough at room temperature
1 egg white, beaten
2 teaspoons vanilla extract, divided
1 1/2 cups heavy cream, divided
3 teaspoons root beer extract

Preheat oven to 350 degrees.

Soak sticks in water for 15 minutes. On a lightly floured surface, roll dough out to $1/8$-inch thickness. Use a $2 1/2$-inch cookie cutter shape to cut dough bottoms. Place bottoms on a lightly greased baking sheet and push sticks into bottoms. Use leftover dough to cover tips of sticks. Prick dough with a fork. Mix together egg white and 1 teaspoon vanilla and brush dough. Bake for 13–15 minutes, or until golden brown. Remove from oven and cool on a wire rack.

In a medium bowl, whip 1 cup cream and root beer extract together until smooth, light, and fluffy. Spoon flavored cream into a pastry bag with a wide tip and pipe onto pops.

In a small bowl, whip remaining $1/2$ cup cream and remaining vanilla together until fluffy. Garnish each pie pop with a dollop of whipped topping. Refrigerate until ready to serve.

BUTTERSCOTCH

~ MAKES 20–25 ~

20–25 wooden sticks
1 9-inch refrigerated pie dough, at room temperature
1 egg white, beaten
3 tablespoons cornstarch
1 cup heavy cream
1 cup brown sugar
1 cup butterscotch morsels, divided
1 tablespoon butter
1 teaspoon vanilla extract
1 egg yolk, beaten, at room temperature
Whipped topping

Preheat oven to 350 degrees.

Soak sticks in water for 15 minutes. On a lightly floured surface, roll dough out to $1/8$-inch thickness. Use a $2^1/2$-inch cookie cutter shape to cut dough bottoms. Place bottoms on a lightly greased baking sheet and push sticks into bottoms. Use leftover dough to cover tips of sticks. Prick dough with fork and brush with egg white. Bake for 14–15 minutes, or until golden brown. Remove from oven and cool on a wire rack.

In a medium saucepan, combine cornstarch, cream, and sugar. Stir over medium heat until sugar has dissolved. Add $1/2$ cup butterscotch morsels, butter, and vanilla. Slowly add egg yolk and simmer for 1 minute stirring constantly. Whisk until mixture is smooth and thick. Remove from heat and set aside to cool. When cooled, add mixture to a pastry bag with a medium tip and pipe onto each pop.

In a small saucepan, melt remaining $1/2$ cup butterscotch morsels, stirring constantly until smooth. Remove from heat and immediately pour melted butterscotch into a candy mold sheet of choice. Place mold in freezer for about 10 minutes, remove, and pop out frozen butterscotch pieces. Garnish pops with whipped topping and butterscotch candy. Refrigerate until ready to serve.

BERRY LUSCIOUS

~ MAKES 14–16 ~

14–16 white lollipop sticks
1 9-inch refrigerated pie dough, at room temperature
3 tablespoons brown sugar
1/2 teaspoon cinnamon
2 tablespoons cornstarch
2 tablespoons butter, softened
1 cup blueberries, washed and drained
2 teaspoons fresh squeezed lemon juice
1 egg white, beaten
Turbinado sugar

Preheat oven to 325 degrees.

On a lightly floured surface, roll dough out to $1/8$-inch thickness. Use a $2 1/2$-inch star shaped cookie cutter to cut out dough tops and bottoms. Use a 1-inch star shaped cookie cutter to cut out a center opening in dough tops. Reserve cutout shapes. Place bottoms on a lightly greased baking sheet and push sticks into bottoms.

In a small saucepan over medium heat, mix together sugar, cinnamon, and cornstarch; stir and simmer for 5 minutes until sugar dissolves. Add butter in very small chunks. Remove from heat and let cool slightly. Fold in berries and add lemon juice.

Add 1 tablespoon of blueberry mixture to center of each dough bottom. Place tops over the blueberry mixture and use a fork to crimp edges together. Place star cutouts over center openings. Brush with egg white and sprinkle with Turbinado sugar.

Bake for 14–15 minutes, watching closely so filling doesn't boil over. Remove from oven and cool on a wire rack.

15–20 wooden sticks
1 9-inch refrigerated pie dough, at room temperature
1 egg white, beaten
1 cup cooked mashed yams or sweet potatoes
2 eggs
½ cup brown sugar
1 teaspoon orange extract
2 teaspoons lemon juice
½ cup heavy cream
¼ teaspoon cinnamon
¼ teaspoon allspice
¼ teaspoon nutmeg
Maple syrup

Preheat oven to 350 degrees.

Soak sticks in water for 15 minutes. On a lightly floured surface, roll dough out to ⅛-inch thickness. Use a 2½-inch maple leaf shaped cookie cutter to cut out dough tops and bottoms. Use a 1-inch cookie cutter shape to cut out a center opening in dough tops. Place bottoms on a lightly greased baking sheet and push sticks into bottoms.

In a medium bowl, combine yams, eggs, and sugar. Add the orange extract, lemon juice, cream, and spices. Use an electric mixer to whip mixture to a light and fluffy consistency. Spoon 1 tablespoon of mixture in the center of each bottom. Place tops over filling and crimp edges together with a fork.

Bake for 12–14 minutes, or until golden brown. Remove from oven and cool on a wire rack. Drizzle with maple syrup.

GRaND Pecan

~ MAKES 14–16 ~

14–16 Popsicle sticks
½ cup brown sugar
2 tablespoons cornstarch
2 tablespoons butter
2 eggs
¼ teaspoon vanilla extract
1 tablespoon Grand Marnier Liqueur or orange extract
1 9-inch refrigerated pie dough, at room temperature
15–20 pecans, chopped
1 egg white, beaten
Maple syrup

Preheat oven to 350 degrees.

Soak sticks in water for 15 minutes. In a large bowl, combine sugar, cornstarch, and butter with an electric mixer until crumbly. Add the eggs and blend until smooth. Add the vanilla and liqueur. Mix well and set aside.

On a lightly floured surface, roll dough out to ⅛-inch thickness. Use a 2½-inch cookie cutter shape to cut out dough tops and bottoms. Use a 1-inch cookie cutter shape to cut out a center opening in dough tops. Place bottoms on a lightly greased baking sheet and push sticks into bottoms.

Place a small mound of pecans in the center of each bottom. Lay tops over the pecans, and crimp edges together with a fork. Spoon 1 teaspoon of liqueur mixture over pecans and brush dough edges with egg white. Bake for 15–20 minutes, or until golden brown. Remove from oven and cool on a wire rack. Drizzle tops with maple syrup and refrigerate until ready to serve.

Kahlúa

20–25 wooden sticks
1 9-inch refrigerated pie dough, at room temperature
1 egg white, beaten
1 1/2 cups heavy cream, divided
3 tablespoons Kahlúa liqueur or instant espresso mix
1 (4-ounce) box banana cream cook and serve pudding mix
1 teaspoon almond extract
Cappuccino drink mix

Preheat oven to 350 degrees.

Soak sticks in water for 15 minutes. On a lightly floured surface, roll dough out to 1/8-inch thickness. Use a 2 1/2-inch round cookie cutter to cut dough bottoms. Place bottoms on a lightly greased baking sheet and push sticks into bottoms. Use leftover dough to cover tips of sticks. Brush bottoms with egg white and prick dough with fork. Bake for 14–15 minutes, or until golden brown. Remove from oven and cool on a wire rack.

In a medium saucepan combine 1 cup of cream and Kahlúa over medium heat (the alcohol will evaporate, leaving the flavor). Add pudding mix and stir until you reach a slight boil. Remove from heat and let cool. Pudding should be thick. Spoon pudding into a pastry bag with a medium tip and pipe onto each pop.

In a medium bowl, combine remaining cream and almond extract using an electric mixer on high speed until light and fluffy. Garnish each pop with whipped topping and dust with cappuccino flavored powder. Refrigerate until ready to serve.

amaretto

20–25 wooden sticks
1 9-inch refrigerated pie dough, at room temperature
1 egg white, beaten
1 (4-ounce) box coconut cream cook and serve pudding mix
1 cup half-and-half
3 tablespoons amaretto or 2 tablespoons almond extract
Whipped topping
20–25 maraschino cherries

Preheat oven to 350 degrees.

Soak sticks in water for 15 minutes. On a lightly floured surface, roll dough out to $1/8$-inch thickness. Use a $2^1/2$-inch heart shaped cookie cutter to cut dough bottoms. Place bottoms on a lightly greased baking sheet and push sticks into bottoms. Use leftover dough to cover tips of sticks. Brush dough with egg white and prick with fork. Bake for 12–14 minutes or until slightly golden brown. Remove from oven and cool on a wire rack.

In a medium saucepan, whisk together pudding mix and half-and-half over medium heat. Mix in the amaretto and bring to a full boil stirring constantly (the alcohol will evaporate, leaving the flavor). Remove from heat and set aside to cool. Spoon the cooled mixture into a pastry bag with a medium tip and pipe onto each pop. Garnish with whipped topping and a cherry. Refrigerate until ready to serve.

MR. BAILEY'S

~ MAKES 20-25 ~

20–25 wooden sticks
1 9-inch refrigerated pie dough, at room temperature
1 cup heavy cream
3 tablespoons cornstarch
1 cup white chocolate chips
3 tablespoons Bailey's liqueur or Bailey's coffee creamer
1 (1.55-ounce) Hershey's Milk Chocolate bar
Whipped topping

Preheat oven to 350 degrees.

Soak sticks in water for 15 minutes. On a lightly floured surface, roll dough out to $1/8$-inch thickness. Use a $2^1/2$-inch cookie cutter shape to cut dough bottoms. Place bottoms on a lightly greased baking sheet and push sticks into bottoms. Use leftover dough to cover tips of sticks. Bake for 12–14 minutes, or until slightly golden brown. Remove from oven and cool on a wire rack.

In a medium saucepan, whisk together the cream and cornstarch over medium heat, stirring constantly to prevent burning. Add chocolate chips and continue stirring until chocolate starts to melt. Add the Bailey's and continue cooking and stirring over low heat for 5 minutes until thick (the alcohol will evaporate, leaving the flavor). Remove from heat and set aside to cool.

Spoon the cooled mixture into a pastry bag with a medium tip and pipe onto each pop. Use a cheese grater or cheese slicer to create chocolate shavings from the chocolate bar. Garnish each pop with whipped topping and chocolate shavings. Refrigerate until ready to serve.

Margarita Rose

20–25 white lollipop sticks
1 9-inch refrigerated pie dough, at room temperature
1 egg white, beaten
1 (4-ounce) box French vanilla instant pudding mix
1 cup heavy cream
3 tablespoons Margarita Rose Strawberry Cream Liqueur, optional
1 cup chopped strawberries
8 ounces melting chocolate

Preheat oven to 350 degrees.

On a lightly floured surface, roll dough out to $1/8$-inch thickness. Use a $2 1/2$-inch round cookie cutter to cut dough bottoms. Place bottoms on a lightly greased baking sheet and push sticks into bottoms. Use leftover dough to cover tips of sticks. Brush with egg white and prick dough with fork. Bake for 12–14 minutes, or until slightly golden brown. Remove from oven and cool on a wire rack.

In a medium bowl, combine pudding mix, cream, and liqueur with electric mixer until thickened. Fold strawberries into pudding mixture. Spoon pudding into a pastry bag with a medium tip and pipe onto pops. In a small microwave-safe bowl, melt chocolate for 2 minutes stirring every 20 seconds until smooth. Add melted chocolate to desired candy mold sheet and place in freezer for 15 minutes to harden. Remove from freezer and pop out chocolate pieces. Garnish pie pops with chocolate pieces. Refrigerate until ready to serve.

S'MORES

15–18 Popsicle sticks
1 9-inch refrigerated pie dough, at room temperature
1/2 cup heavy cream
1/2 cup milk
8 ounces semisweet chocolate chips
1 egg, beaten
2 cups mini marshmallows
Chocolate sauce, optional

Preheat oven to 350 degrees.

Soak sticks in water for 15 minutes. On a lightly floured surface, roll dough out to 1/8-inch thickness. Use a 2 1/2-inch square cookie cutter to cut out dough tops and bottoms. Use a 1-inch cookie cutter shape to cut out a center opening in dough tops. Place bottoms on a lightly greased baking sheet and push sticks into bottoms.

In a medium saucepan, combine cream and milk over medium heat. Add the chocolate chips and stir until completely melted. Slowly add the egg stirring constantly until mixture is smooth and thick. Simmer for 1 minute and remove from heat.

Place 1 tablespoon of chocolate mixture in the center of each dough bottom. Place tops over chocolate and crimp edges together with a fork. Bake for 18–20 minutes, or until golden brown. Remove from oven and cool on a wire rack.

Garnish tops with marshmallows and return to oven on broiler setting keeping a close watch until marshmallows start to brown. Remove from oven and serve immediately. Drizzle with chocolate sauce if using.

GReeN SLIME

20–25 wooden sticks
1 9-inch refrigerated pie dough, at room temperature
1 (7.5-ounce) package Southern Gourmet Key Lime Pie filling
2 egg yolks
2 ⅓ cups water
1 (0.75-ounce) tube green gel frosting

Preheat oven to 350 degrees.

Soak sticks in water for 15 minutes. On a lightly floured surface, roll dough out to $\frac{1}{8}$-inch thickness. Use a $2\frac{1}{2}$-inch cookie cutter shape to cut dough bottoms. Place bottoms on a lightly greased baking sheet and push sticks into bottoms. Use leftover dough to cover tips of sticks. Bake for 12–14 minutes, or until slightly golden brown. Remove from oven and cool on a wire rack.

In a medium saucepan, prepare pie filling according to package directions using the egg yolks and water. Set aside and let cool. When cooled, spoon mix into a pastry bag with a medium tip and pipe onto pops. Garnish tops with a swirl of gel frosting. Refrigerate until ready to serve.

HOPSCOTCH

~ MAKES 15–18 ~

15–18 wooden sticks
1 9-inch refrigerated pie dough, at room temperature
1 cup butterscotch chips
1 cup brown sugar
½ cup light corn syrup

Preheat oven to 350 degrees.

Soak sticks in water for 15 minutes. On a lightly floured surface, roll dough out to ⅛-inch thickness. Use various 2½-inch cookie cutter shapes to cut out dough tops and bottoms. Use a 1-inch cookie cutter shape to cut out a center opening in dough tops. Place bottoms on a lightly greased baking sheet and push sticks into bottoms.

In a medium saucepan, stir together butterscotch chips and sugar over medium heat until smooth. Add syrup and continue to stir and cook for 5 more minutes. Mixture will thicken as it cools. Place 1 tablespoon of butterscotch mixture in center of each bottom. Cover with dough top and crimp edges together with a fork. Bake for 15–16 minutes. Butterscotch will cook through the openings and crust will turn golden brown. Remove from oven and cool on a wire rack.

Oreo

20–25 Popsicle sticks
½ cup finely crushed Oreo cookies, cream fillings removed
1 cup flour
1 teaspoon salt
7 tablespoons cold unsalted butter, cubed
1½ tablespoons ice cold water
1 cup heavy cream
1 teaspoon vanilla extract
¼ cup Southern Gourmet Vanilla Mousse mix
20–25 mini Oreo cookies

Preheat oven to 325 degrees.

Soak sticks in water for 15 minutes. Combine crushed cookies, flour, and salt in bowl of food processor using the pulse setting. Add the butter and pulse until mixture is crumbly. Gradually add the water and pulse mixture about 5 more times until ingredients come together as dough. Remove from food processor and work dough on a floured surface. Dough might be very sticky, so be sure to have enough flour on hand to prevent sticking to surface and rolling pin.

Roll out dough to a ⅙-inch thickness; it needs to be thicker than regular pie dough. Use a 2½-inch round cookie cutter to cut dough bottoms. Place bottoms on a lightly greased baking sheet and push sticks into bottoms. Use leftover dough to cover tips of sticks. Bake for 10–11 minutes; do not overcook. They are ready when they begin to look like little cookies. Remove from oven and cool on a wire rack.

In a medium bowl, combine cream, vanilla, and mousse mix with a hand mixer until light and fluffy. Spoon mixture into a pastry bag with a medium tip and pipe onto pops. Garnish with mini Oreo cookies. Refrigerate until ready to serve.

Nutty Nutella

15–20 hobby craft sticks
1 9-inch refrigerated pie dough, at room temperature
$\frac{1}{2}$ cup Nutella spread
$\frac{1}{2}$ teaspoon cinnamon
1 tablespoon light corn syrup
Powdered Sugar Icing (page 11), optional
Chocolate shavings or finely chopped nuts, optional

Preheat oven to 325 degrees.

Soak sticks in water for 15 minutes. On a lightly floured surface, roll dough out to $\frac{1}{8}$-inch thickness. Use a $2\frac{1}{2}$-inch animal shaped cookie cutter to cut out dough tops and bottoms. Use a smaller cookie cutter shape to cut out a center opening in dough tops. Place bottoms on a lightly greased baking sheet and push sticks into bottoms.

In a small bowl, combine Nutella, cinnamon, and syrup. Add 1 rounded teaspoon of mixture to center of each bottom. Place tops over mixture and crimp edges together with a fork. Bake for 14 minutes, or until golden brown. Remove from oven to a wire rack and drizzle tops with Powdered Sugar Frosting while still warm. Garnish with chocolate shavings or nuts.

Nilla

20–25 wooden sticks
1 9-inch refrigerated pie dough, at room temperature
1 teaspoon vanilla extract
1 egg white
1 cup heavy cream
$\frac{1}{2}$ cup French vanilla instant pudding mix
20–25 mini vanilla wafers
Powdered Sugar Icing (page 11)

Preheat oven to 350 degrees.

Soak sticks in water for 15 minutes. On a lightly floured surface, roll dough out to $\frac{1}{8}$-inch thickness. Use a $2\frac{1}{2}$-inch flower shaped cookie cutter to cut dough bottoms. Place bottoms on a lightly greased baking sheet and push sticks into bottoms. Use leftover dough to cover tips of sticks. In a small bowl, beat together vanilla and egg white; brush over bottoms and prick dough with a fork. Bake for 14–15 minutes, or until golden brown. Remove from oven and cool on a wire rack.

In a medium bowl, combine cream and pudding mix. Beat with an electric mixer on high speed until light and fluffy. Spoon mixture into a pastry bag with a medium tip and pipe onto each pop. Top with mini vanilla wafers and drizzle with icing. Refrigerate until ready to serve.

chocolate TURtles

18–20 Popsicle sticks
½ cup finely crushed Oreo cookies, cream fillings removed
1 cup flour
1 teaspoon salt
7 tablespoons cold unsalted butter, cubed
1½ tablespoons ice cold water
1 cup semisweet chocolate chips
½ cup chopped nuts
1 (4-ounce) box butterscotch instant pudding mix
1 cup heavy cream

Preheat oven to 325 degrees.

Soak sticks in water for 15 minutes. Combine crushed cookies, flour, and salt in bowl of food processor, using the pulse setting. Add the cold butter and pulse until mixture is crumbly. Add the ice cold water gradually and pulse mixture about 5 more times until ingredients come together as dough. Remove from food processor and work dough on a floured surface. Dough might be very sticky, so be sure to have enough flour on hand to prevent sticking to surface and rolling pin.

Roll out dough to a $\frac{1}{6}$-inch thickness; it needs to be thicker than regular pie dough. Use a $2\frac{1}{2}$-inch round or turtle shaped cookie cutter to cut dough bottoms. Place bottoms on a lightly greased baking sheet and push sticks into bottoms. Use leftover dough to cover tips of sticks and to make the turtle legs and head. Bake for 10–11 minutes; do not overcook. Remove from oven and cool on a wire rack.

Melt chocolate in a small microwave-safe bowl for 2 minutes on high, stirring every 20 seconds until smooth. Add nuts to bottom of individual candy molds if desired and then pour melted chocolate over top. Place molds in freezer for about 10 minutes to set. Pop candies out and set aside.

In a medium bowl, beat together pudding mix and cream with an electric mixer on high speed until it thickens. Place 1 tablespoon of filling on each pie pop and garnish with chocolate pieces. Refrigerate until ready to serve.

TiGER'S BLOOD

~ MAKES 25–30 ~

25–30 wooden sticks
1 9-inch refrigerated pie dough, at room temperature
1 (15-ounce) can cherry pie filling, chopped
1 egg white, beaten
Powdered Sugar Icing (page 11)

Preheat oven to 350 degrees.

Soak sticks in water for 15 minutes. On a lightly floured surface, roll dough out to $^{1}/_{8}$-inch thickness. Use a $2^{1}/_{2}$-inch round cookie cutter to cut out dough tops and bottoms. Place bottoms on a lightly greased baking sheet and push sticks into bottoms. Prick bottoms with a fork.

Place 1 teaspoon of pie filling in the center of each dough bottom. Don't overfill or filling will boil out. Be sure to leave a clean edge around the dough bottom for a good closure. Add tops and crimp edges together with a fork. Use a paring knife to make slits in the dough tops for steam vents. Brush with egg white.

Bake for 15–16 minutes, or until golden brown. Remove from oven and cool on a wire rack. Drizzle with Powdered Sugar Icing while still warm.

PBJ

15–20 Popsicle sticks
1 9-inch refrigerated pie dough, at room temperature
Creamy peanut butter
Grape jelly

Preheat oven to 325 degrees.

Soak sticks in water for 15 minutes. On a lightly floured surface, roll dough out to $1/8$-inch thickness. Use a $2^1/2$-inch animal shaped cookie cutter to cut out dough tops and bottoms. Use a smaller $1/2$-inch cookie cutter shape to cut a center opening in dough tops. Place bottoms on a lightly greased baking sheet and push sticks into bottoms.

Place small amounts of peanut butter and jelly in center of each bottom. Add tops and crimp edges together with a fork. Bake for 10–12 minutes, keeping watch so that the jelly doesn't bubble over.

SPOOKY

~ MAKES 15–20 ~

15–20 wooden sticks
1 9-inch refrigerated pie dough, at room temperature
1 cup canned pumpkin puree
1 (4-ounce) box vanilla instant pudding mix
1 teaspoon cinnamon
1/4 teaspoon ground ginger
1/4 teaspoon ground nutmeg
Powdered Sugar Icing (page 11)

Preheat oven to 350 degrees.

Soak sticks in water for 15 minutes. On a lightly floured surface, roll dough out to 1/8-inch thickness. Use a 2 1/2-inch cookie cutter shape to cut out dough tops and bottoms. Use a 1-inch cookie cutter shape to cut out a center opening in dough tops. Place bottoms on a lightly greased baking sheet and push sticks into bottoms.

In a small bowl, combine pumpkin and pudding mix. Add spices and mix thoroughly. Place 1 tablespoon of pumpkin mixture in center of each bottom. Add tops and crimp edges together with a fork. Bake for 17–18 minutes. Pumpkin may cook through the opening and crust will be golden brown. Remove from oven and cool on wire rack. Drizzle with Powdered Sugar Icing and refrigerate until ready to serve.

METRIC CONVERSION CHART

Volume Measurements		Weight Measurements		Temperature Conversion	
U.S.	**Metric**	**U.S.**	**Metric**	**Fahrenheit**	**Celsius**
1 teaspoon	5 ml	1/2 ounce	15 g	250	120
1 tablespoon	15 ml	1 ounce	30 g	300	150
1/4 cup	60 ml	3 ounces	90 g	325	160
1/3 cup	75 ml	4 ounces	115 g	350	180
1/2 cup	125 ml	8 ounces	225 g	375	190
2/3 cup	150 ml	12 ounces	350 g	400	200
3/4 cup	175 ml	1 pound	450 g	425	220
1 cup	250 ml	2 1/4 pounds	1 kg	450	230